AN UNREDEEMED CAPTIVE

AN
UNREDEEMED
CAPTIVE

BEING THE STORY OF EUNICE
WILLIAMS, WHO, AT THE AGE
OF SEVEN YEARS, WAS CARRIED
AWAY FROM DEERFIELD BY THE
INDIANS IN THE YEAR 1704, AND
WHO LIVED AMONG THE INDIANS
IN CANADA AS ONE OF THEM
THE REST OF HER LIFE · · · · · ·

WRITTEN BY
CLIFTON JOHNSON
WITH ILLUSTRATIONS BY THE AUTHOR
AND MANY OLD-TIME ENGRAVINGS
MDCCCXCVII

An Indian Scout

AN UNREDEEMED CAPTIVE

By
Clifton Johnson

YE GALLEON PRESS
FAIRFIELD, WASHINGTON
1999

ISBN 0-87770-702-2 pb

INTRODUCTION

As the frontier moved westward and as settlers took over land held for many generations by Native Americans, there were a number of conflicts between them. If the whites won, it was a battle, if the Indians won, it was a massacre. In the conflicts in which Indians won, quite often white men were killed, but Indians were reluctant to kill women and children, so they were sometimes captured and held for ransom. Often an effort was made to adopt white women and children into the tribes, perhaps to replace individuals lost in battles. In a few cases the captives managed to escape and find their way back to civilization. There were those frustrating cases where captives, after a taste of the carefree Indian communal lifestyle, refused to return to the strict New England, God fearing life, preferring to live out the rest of their lives with the native people who had adopted them.

The case of Eunice Williams was especially trying for her family and friends as her mother was killed during captivity and she was kept with the tribe instead of being ransomed. She married a Native American and worst of all had converted to the Catholic faith. Decades later, she returned to visit Deerfield, Massachusetts where she had been taken prisoner in 1704, but she still refused to return permanently. By this time she had forgotten her English speech and could only converse through an interpreter. When white women bore Indian children which of course happened in a number of cases including this one, they knew that the children would be accepted in the Indian society but would not be accepted in white society.

French people had settled in along the St. Lawrence River in what is now Canada before the

Pilgrims landed in Massachusetts. With them came their Catholic priests determined to save red man souls or die in the attempt. In 1704 the frontier was the Connecticut Valley. Later it was the Ohio Valley, then on to the northern Great Plains, and next to the Pacific. Mile by mile, the Indians were pushed back, always to the poorest of land. Treaties were made with a minority of the tribe members where whites attempted to gain control of land, disregarding the wishes of the majority of a tribe.

Living on the frontier in isolated log cabins where Indian raids were a possible danger, made capture by red men an occupational hazard. A good many white women were made captive over the decades and no doubt some were mistreated. For every case of mistreatment by Indian males there probably were a hundred cases where white men took advantage of Indian women. In the case of Eunice Williams, from all accounts, entered willingly in a marriage with an Indian man in a union presided over by a Catholic priest. This seems to have been a long lasting relationship where each remained loyal to the other. In the years following she gave birth to his children. The exact number of children she had is unknown, reported to have been up to eight, but not all of them lived. We know that at least two of them, both boys, lived to maturity, married, and so left descendants in the St. Lawrence region.

An Unredeemed Captive

Chapter I

Of the Settlement of Deerfield—John Eliot and
the Indians—The Purchase of the Deerfield
Grant from the Savages by Major Pynchon
— The First Minister and the First Tavern

THE old French and Indian wars
began in the year 1689 and continued with only two or three short
intermissions of peace until 1763. During all this long period of seventy-
four years the weakling colonies of
New England were constantly harassed
by raiding parties of the enemy; and
it is probable no English town in the
colonies suffered more in the struggle
for race supremacy from the depreda-
tions of the French and Indians than
Old Deerfield. It was one of the New
England outposts and its position in the
Connecticut valley made it easy of access
by one of the natural routes from the

north. Once it was all but wiped out, and the inhabitants of the region, singly or several at a time, continued to be shot or captured by the northern enemy down to 1758. But this does not include all

its troubles from savage foes, for its first experience of war dated back to the time of the Indian rising under King Philip.

Deerfield was an offshoot of Dedham, one of the old towns a few miles out from Boston. This connection with Dedham came about indirectly through John

Eliot, the famous apostle to the Indians. The conversion of the natives was early an object of solicitude among the almost morbidly religious Puritans. But the obstacles were such that the work was not begun in earnest till 1644. It was in the autumn of that year that John Eliot, the scholarly pastor of the church at Roxbury, preached his first sermon in the Indian tongue in a wigwam on Nonantum Hill. From this time to the end of his life his labors for the Indians were unflagging. He soon saw that as long as the Indians remained in their savage state, living in scattered groups and frequently moving from place to place, the results he accomplished would be transient and uncertain, and he says he " looked for some spot somewhat remote from the English, where the Word might be constantly taught, and government constantly exercised, means of good sub-sistence provided," etc.

Such a site he found at Natick. The General Court approved the scheme and the town of Dedham turned over 2000 acres of land to the Indians. The bounds for the Indian plantation at Natick were duly laid out, but, just as in all the history of the whites' dealings with the natives when they own land the whites covet, the years following were noisy with complaints of " affronts offered " by the savages and disputes about the lines of separation. In the end, to compensate the Dedhamites for their supposed losses and sufferings at the hands of their Indian neighbors, the General Court granted them 8000 acres of land which they were to pick out wherever they chose in the yet unsettled parts of the colony.

The selectmen, to whom the matter was turned over, looked about and presently "heard of a considerable tract of good land that might be answerable to the town's expectation, about ten or twelve miles north from Hadley;" and they advised that the town should take possession "with all convenient speed, before any other granter enter upon it and prevent us."

In 1665 the bounds of the grant had

been determined and the next thing to be done was to go through the farce of purchasing it from the Indians.   All the land occupied by our New England settlers was bought from the Indians, but the early pioneers never let sentiment interfere with business — they bought as cheaply as they could, independent of the real worth of their purchases.   For instance, all the fertile lowlands from Suffield to Northfield were obtained

from the natives for a few great coats and some hundred fathoms of wampum. The Indians were as children in the hands of the Puritans when it came to business.

Major John Pynchon of Springfield,

in his double capacity of magistrate and trader, had much to do with local Indians and effected nearly every important purchase from them. The Sachems of the valley kept a running account at Pynchon's shop, and to offset this account they pledged their lands in payment. Here are the items of a bill against Umpachala, the Norwottuck Sachem, in payment of which the Indian gave Pynchon a deed of the town of Hadley :

	£	s.	d.
2 coats, shag and wampum	5		
Red shag cotton, knife		7	
Wampum and 2 coats	5	10	
a kettle	1	5	
for your being drunk		10	

The total is $64. It is no wonder if the Indians on reflection wanted to scalp such traders and their associates. Technically there was no injustice, but advantage was taken of the fact that the red man, with his simple wants and characteristic lack of foresight, was no match for the ambition and shrewdness of the civilized white.

It was to Major Pynchon that the Dedham authorities looked to get them a clear title to their tract of land from the original owners. This he did with his usual economy, only reserving to the natives the right "of fishing in the waters and rivers, and free liberty to hunt deer and other wild creatures, and to gather walnuts, chestnuts and other nuts and things on the commons."

The Deerfield grant was duly divided among the Dedham townspeople and in a few cases the new owners emigrated to their wilderness property. In the main, however, they held the land as a speculation, just as a person might now possess himself of suburban lots to be sold when he saw a chance to make a satisfactory profit.

Two Hatfield men were the first to put up their rude abodes in the forests that then covered the site of the new town. This was in the early summer of 1670. Others followed, and in a few years the settlement had grown to quite a village, the houses dotted along on a

north and south line in almost exactly
the same place and manner as in the
town of the present.

In 1673, the General Court granted
the Deerfield settlers such an addition
to the original 8000 acres as should
make them a township seven miles
square, provided that within three years
they should settle "an able and orthodox
minister." The frontier citizens did not
await the time limit; for that same year
Mr. Samuel Mather began his labors
as the first minister of Deerfield. He

was then only twenty-two years old, a recent graduate of Harvard College and a near relative of those two New England notables, Increase and Cotton Mather.

With the church thus established, the only thing that remained to fully round out the town life was a tavern. This came the year following, when Moses Crafts "was licensed to keep an Ordinary and to sell wines and strong liquors for one year, provided he kept good order in his house." Drinking was far more general in those days than now and the alehouse was inevitable, but it is to be noted that the church preceded it. In the story of our western country it is a different matter. There the saloon has always marched in the vanguard of civilization.

At first the town was known by its Indian name of Pocumtuck, but the abundance of deer in its woodlands suggested, and in time gave, its present name acceptance. The savages still hunted, trapped and fished in the valley, they bartered at the tavern or made small ex-

changes of mats and baskets for civilized
wares at the village housedoors, and their
wigwams were to be seen along the
streamsides as of old.   There was peace
in the valley and the new settlers were
beginning to conquer comfort and pros-
perity.

Chapter II

Of King Philip's War — Deerfield Destroyed —
The Settlement Again Begun — Rev. John
Williams Becomes the Second Minister —
Eunice Williams Is Born, 1696 — Her Life
as a Child

NOW there rose the cloud of war — a
war of barbarism resisting the en-
croachments of civilization. It started
with Philip, sachem of the Wampanoags,
who burned the village of Swanzey and
three other villages of Plymouth Colony
and murdered many of the inhabitants.

By this time the Indians had acquired
a good many firearms and become expert
in the use of them, so that they were
not so unequal a match for the whites
as formerly. The Wampanoags were
soon put down, but Philip escaped to
the Nipmucks of Worcester County, and
these savages carried on the war for a
year, burning and slaughtering all the
way from the Connecticut River, then

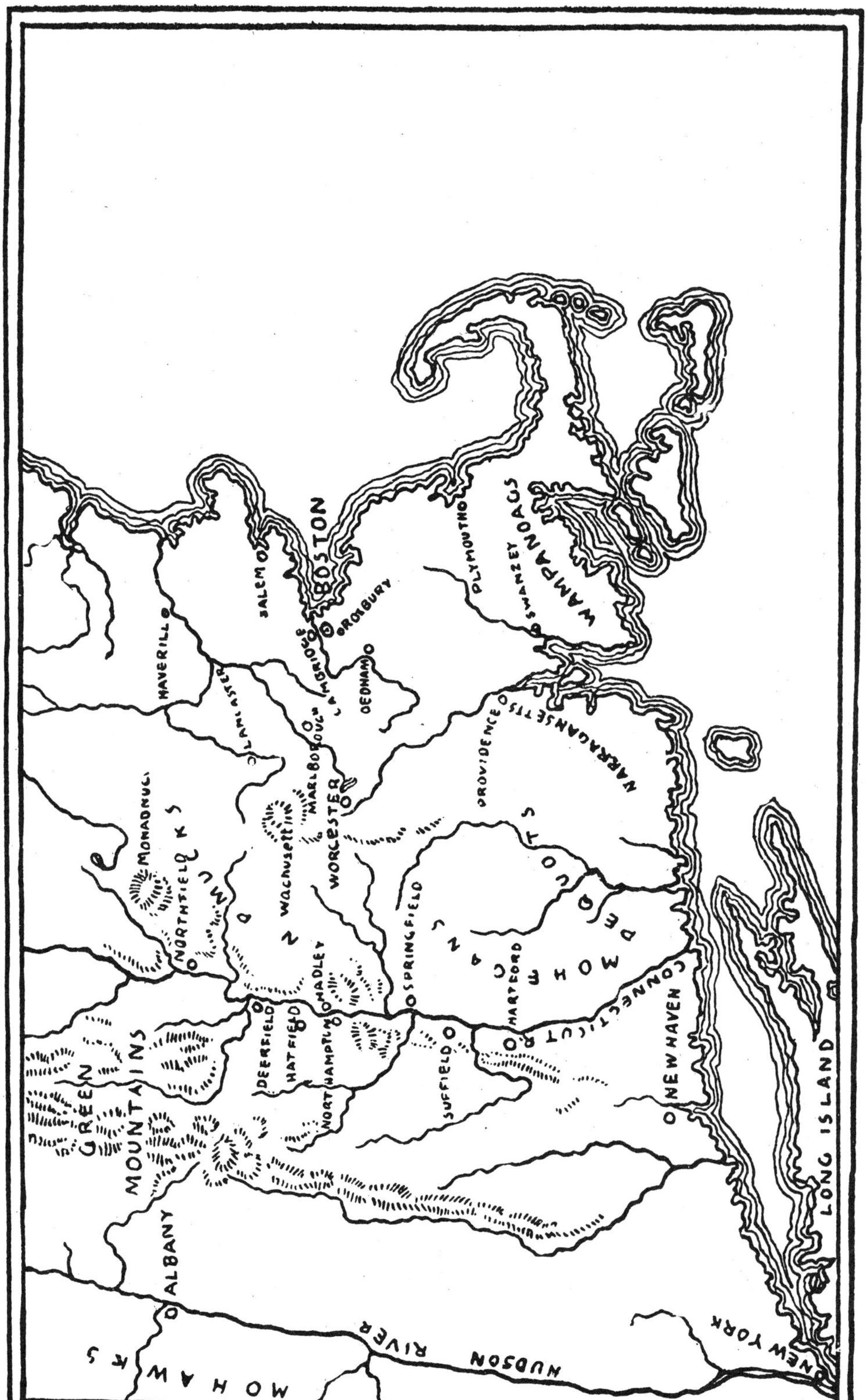
BOSTON
SALEM
ROXBURY
CAMBRIDGE
DEDHAM
PLYMOUTH
SWANZEY
WAMPANOAGS
HAVERILL
LANCASTER
MARLBOROUGH
WORCESTER
PROVIDENCE
NARRAGANSETTS
MONADNUC
NORTHFIELD
NIPMUCKS
Wachusett
SPRINGFIELD
PEQUOTS
MOHEGANS
HARTFORD
CONNECTICUT R.
DEERFIELD
HATFIELD
HADLEY
NORTHAMPTON
SUFFIELD
NEW HAVEN
GREEN MOUNTAINS
ALBANY
MOHAWKS
HUDSON RIVER
NEW YORK
LONG ISLAND

the western frontier, to within a dozen miles of Boston. In the end, the whites conquered and the greater number of the enemy was killed, while the rest were sold as slaves in the West Indies and elsewhere.

Philip himself was ambushed and shot and the chieftain's hands were shown as a spectacle in Boston, while his ghastly head was set up on a pole in Plymouth, affording the occasion for a public thanksgiving.

Scarcely any Indians were left in New England except the friendly Mohegans. The brunt of the savage attacks was borne by the colonies of Massachusetts and Plymouth. Of ninety towns, twelve had been utterly destroyed, while more than forty had been the scene of fire and massacre. More than a thousand men had been slain, and a great many women and children.

In the view of the majority of our ancestors, who lived in that day, this devastation had a religious aspect, and the preachers admonished their flocks that these sufferings were directly due to their sins. We find Parson Stoddard of Northampton writing to Increase Mather that "many sins are so grown in fashion that it is a question whether they be sins," and begs him to call the governor's attention to "that intolerable pride in clothes and hair, and the toleration of so many taverns; and suffering home dwellers to be tippling therein." His conclusion is that "it would be a dreadful token of the displeasure of God if these afflictions pass away without much spiritual advantage."

Deerfield was one of the sufferers in King Philip's war. It was attacked on September 1st, 1675, several houses were burned and one man killed. After that the inhabitants huddled together in two or three houses, poorly protected by palisades and defended by a handful of soldiers. Many of them piled their household goods on their ox carts and wended their way through the forests to the larger settlements down the river. At Hadley there was a strong garrison

King Philip—From an Old Print

which presently began to feel the need
of provisions, and in the middle of September, Captain Lathrop with eighty men,
besides teamsters and carts, went up to

Deerfield to secure the grain which the
settlers had there harvested and stacked.
It was on their return with the threshed
grain that the famous massacre of Bloody
Brook occurred, when all but a scant half
dozen of the company were slaughtered
by the savages.

Soon after this disaster, the garrison
was withdrawn from Deerfield and the
Indians burned what was left of the

plantation. Several attempts were made to rebuild the village in the following years, but the savages were continually lurking about; more lives were lost, the new buildings were fired, and it was not till 1682 that the settlement was again made permanent. But the enterprise of our wilderness pioneers had been so paralyzed by the reverses and frights of the past that the growth of the hamlet was very slow.

It was six years before they again had a minister. Their choice was John Williams, then but little more than twenty-one years of age. On their part his parishioners agreed to give their minister a home-lot and 220 acres of meadow land. Also, they would build him a house 42 feet long, 20 feet wide, with a lean-to at the rear; would fence his home-lot, and within two years build him a barn and break up his ploughing land. For yearly salary he was to have sixty pounds. This was largely paid in produce, such as wheat, peas, Indian corn and pork.

Soon after his ordination Mr. Williams married a young Northampton woman, and in the next sixteen years there were born to them eleven children. Of these, the sixth child and second daughter was born September 17th, 1696, and was named Eunice, after her mother. She it is who is the subject of this little book. She lived the simple life of the other village children, with its round of work and play, church-going and attending school. She was quick in her studies and became a good reader, and under the double drill at school and home early memorized the catechism. She looked with interest at the tavern when she passed it, half fearfully, for she reflected the home sentiment that it was a place with a decided flavor of ungodliness. Once, in the dusk of a summer evening, she saw two teamsters on the porch, using loud, rude words, and one shook his fist in the other's face, whereat her opinion of the tavern's badness was confirmed, and she ran home in great fright.

On the other hand, she liked to loiter at the door of Deacon French's blacksmith shop. That was a place of peace and sobriety, and it was a pleasant sight to see the sparks dance about and hear the metal ring as the Deacon wielded his hammer. The parsonage, with a number of other humble dwellings in the village center, was inclosed by a palisade that included within it about twenty acres. Outside the palisade, the little girl was not allowed to go unless accompanied by one of her elders. But this fence of stout posts with their pointed tops interested her, and she knew the whole line of it, and she often

The Fort-house

peeked through the chinks of it out into
the surrounding woods and clearings.
Here and there she could see stockaded
dwellings, and she knew that some of
her mates in the village school lived in
them. It was a strange world, this
woodland country outside the palisades.
She had heard many stories of the
Indians and of the wild creatures of the
forest, and she, herself, when walking
with her hand in her father's, on the
way to make a pastoral call at a house
beyond the village defences, had seen
three deer feeding in a stumpy clearing.

Near the northwest angle of the pali-
saded part of the village stood the meet-
ing-house, homely and square with a
four-sided roof crowned by a tiny belfry.
Close by the church was a heavily-built
garrison house with an overhanging
upper story and loopholes from which
guns might be fired. Eunice knew that
in case the Indians attacked them and
carried the palisade, it was to this stout
fort-house the people would retreat. She
knew how the Indians had burned the

town years before and the stories she heard made her fearful of every shadow when she stepped outdoors after sun-down. Often at bedtime she felt such fright that she would draw the clothes over her head and catch her breath at every sound.

Chapter III

Of the Renewal of War — Mr. Williams' Apprehension and the Warning of Col. Schuyler — The Superstitions of the Times — The Winter March of the Invaders — The Bell of St. Regis — The Attack on the Town — The Old Indian House

AS has been said France and England were for nearly three-quarters of a century almost continually at war, and there was a feeling of intense hostility between their colonies over the seas, even when there was no armed expedition in the field. Under the pretext of protecting the eastern Indians from English encroachment the French were constantly inciting them to marauding the New England frontiers. In 1703 plans were laid to cut off the outlying English settlements from one end of New England to the other, but these plans were not fully executed. Many eastern settlements were destroyed, but those on the

western borders remained unmolested
It is true there were rumors of an expedition against Deerfield, and Rev. Mr.
Williams was so apprehensive of danger
that he applied to the government of
the province to detail a guard for the
town, on which twenty soldiers were sent
for a garrison. Besides, the minister
sufficiently roused his people so that
they strengthened the fortifications, but
the danger was not as clearly realized as
it should have been.

What was known of the intentions of
the enemy came from Col. John Schuyler
at Albany, who was in the habit of get-
ting such intelligence from the Indians
trading in that place. The Indians who
furnished him information were Mohawks
who knew of Canadian affairs through a
band of their relatives settled at what
was then called Saint Louis, now Caughnawaga, nine miles above Montreal. The
latter had been converted by the Jesuits
and persuaded to emigrate and settle on
the St. Lawrence where they naturally
allied themselves with the French.

Deerfield, at that time, except for a few families at Northfield, was the most northerly settlement on the Connecticut river. It was perfectly easy for the enemy to approach it unawares, and there was in the air a feeling that some untoward calamity was brewing. It was an age of superstition. Women were

hung for witches in Salem, and witch-craft was believed in everywhere. Did the butter or soap delay their coming, the churn and the kettle were bewitched. Did the chimney refuse to draw, witches

were blowing the smoke down the flue
Did the loaded cart get stuck, invisible
hands were holding it. Did the cow's
milk grow scant, the imps had been suck-
ing her. Did the sick child cry, search
was made for the witches' pins. Ideas
of this sort and the tales told to illus-
trate them so worked on the minds of the
people that adults, as well as children,
were ready to see a ghost in every slip
of moonshine and trace to malign origin
every sound that broke the stillness of
the night — the rattle of a shutter, the
creak of a door, the moan of the winds
or the cries of the beasts and birds.

For two or three evenings previous to
February 29th, 1704, a new topic of su-
pernatural interest had been added to the
usual stock. Ominous sounds had been
heard in the night, and, says Rev. Solo-
mon Stoddard, " the people of Deerfield
were strangely amazed by a trampling
noise around the fort, as if it was besieged
by Indians." The older men recalled simi-
lar omens before the outbreak of Philip's
war, when from the clear sky came the

sound of horses' hoofs, the roar of artil-
lery, the rattle of small arms, and the
beating of drums to the charge. These
tales of fear were in everybody's mouth,
and even the thoughtful were possessed
with an undefinable dread.

At that moment, just beyond the
northern horizon, their foes were on the
southward march bent on overwhelming
the settlement. A horde of Frenchmen
turned half Indian, and savages armed
with civilized powers of destruction were
hurrying towards our doomed frontier
over the dreary waste of snow which
stretched away for hundreds of miles to
the St. Lawrence.

This expedition, under the command
of Hertel de Rouville, advanced by way
of Lake Champlain, which they left near
the present city of Burlington to follow
up the Winooski river. From the head-
waters of this stream they passed through
a gap in the Green Mountains, came
down the valley of White river, then for
a long distance traveled southward on
the frozen Connecticut.

In the dark shades of some ravine, a day's march nearer our border, each night their camp was pitched and kettles hung. Their fires lighted up the mossy trunks and overhanging branches of the giant hemlock and towering pine, throwing their summits into a deeper gloom, and building up a wall of pitchy darkness, which enclosed the camp on every side. A frugal supper, and quiet soon reigned within this circle, and around each camp-fire the tired forms of the invaders were stretched on beds of evergreens, to be up at dawn, and, after a hasty breakfast, onward again.

Dogs with sledges aided to transport the equipage of the camp, and the march was swift. The final day came and dogs, sledges and such baggage as was not needed were left behind, while the army pushed forward over the last miles of the journey with celerity and caution, and reached a pine-clad bluff overlooking the Deerfield Valley on the night of February 28th. Here, behind a low ridge, the packs were unstrapped, the

war paint put on, and all preparations
made.

One tradition has it that the object
that brought these three or four hundred
French and Indians all this winter journey from their northern homes was the
capture of the bell in the village church.
They were moved by righteous indigna-
tion, for this bell had been taken by a
colonial privateer from a French vessel
while on its way to a Catholic church in
Canada. It is said further that the invaders, after securing the bell, dragged
it away on sledges to Canada, and that
there, in a little church in St. Regis, it
calls the worshipers to service to this
day. Several times since its capture, so
the story goes, efforts have been made
by Deerfield people to have the bell returned, and negotiating committees have
made the pilgrimage to St. Regis with
this end in view. But the French will
not part with the bell, and if it ever
comes back it will come as it went — the
spoils of war.

The enemy lay in concealment on the

bleak ridge two miles north of the town till the darkest hour of the night came —that preceding the first grayness of morning. Then they crept in on the sleeping village. It was midwinter and the slight defence of palisades was in many places drifted over with snow. More than that, a stiff crust had formed on the snow sufficient to bear the weight of a man, and the enemy left their snow-shoes behind at the borders of the meadow that intervened between their hiding place and the village. The town sentinels proved unfaithful. They had retired shortly before, and there was no alarm given at the enemy's approach. The savage foe came noiselessly over the palisades at the northwest corner, where the winter winds had lifted the highest drifts, and distributed themselves among the peaceful homes. Then came the dreadful warwhoop, the blows of axes on resisting doors, the leaping of flames and the report of muskets. Only two houses—one within the palisades and another outside—made a successful re-

sistance, and except for the occupants
of these and a few who escaped to the
woods, the rest of the inhabitants were
either killed or captured. There was no
time to fly to the garrison house, in
which lived Captain John Sheldon, for

it was surrounded by the savages in the
first onslaught. Its door was heavily
bolted and the savages, finding they
could not push it in by main force,
hacked a hole with their tomahawks,
then thrust a musket through the aper-
ture and fired and killed the captain's
wife. The captain's son leaped from a
chamber window, gained the shelter of

the woods and escaped to Hatfield. Soon the garrison house fell into the hands of the foe, and as it was one of the largest in the place, they used it as a depot for the prisoners they were fast collecting.

The house that made the stoutest fight was one about fifty yards distant from Sheldon's, where were seven armed men and several women. While the men fired on the savages the women loaded their guns or cast bullets for future use, and after various attempts to take the house by stratagem or burn it, the enemy gave their attention to keeping out of range of the defenders' shot.

At the end of the fight the only two houses within the palisades that were not smoking ruins were the one so bravely defended and the garrison house. The latter had been pillaged, and when the enemy began their retreat they set it on fire, but it was saved by the efforts of the few English who had escaped death and capture and were still in the village. This building, as time went on and the

The Door of the Old Indian House

events of this February night receded
into the past, came to be known as
"The Old Indian House." It stood in
its wonted place till 1848, when in its
mossy and loose-clapboarded old age it
was torn down. Even then its sills and
other timbers were as sound as when
the house was first erected. The old door,
filled with nails and gashed by Indian
tomahawks, has luckily been preserved,
a most interesting relic, with a few other
fragments of the house, in the Deerfield Museum.

Chapter IV

Of the Capture of the Minister's House — The
    Enemy's Retreat — The Death of Mrs. Will-
    iams — Eunice is Treated Kindly by Her
    Indian Captor

ONE of the houses first to be carried
in the assault was that of the Rev.
John Williams. For what we know of
the details of the affray and of the experi-
ences of himself and family in their
captivity, we are indebted to his own
quaint relation of the facts in his " The
Redeemed Captive." This old-time book
was published soon after the reverend
author's return from Canada, and so
great was the interest in his narrative that
six successive editions were called for.

He tells how he was awakened from
his sleep by the violent endeavors of the
enemy to break open doors and windows
with axes and hatchets. No sooner was
he out of bed than he saw that the foe
had already effected an entrance, and he

called to awaken the rest of the household and reached up to the bed-tester
for his pistol. Immediately the enemy
broke into the room, a dozen or twenty
of them "with painted faces and hideous
acclamations." The minister cocked his
pistol and put it to the breast of the
foremost Indian, but the weapon missed
fire and he was seized, disarmed and
bound. Then the savages "insulted over
him awhile, holding up hatchets over his
head and threatening to burn all he had."
His two youngest children and his negro
woman they killed and the others of the
family they huddled into the bedroom
and held as prisoners.

When the sun was an hour high the
pillage and destruction were complete,
thirty-eight of the English had been
killed and 119 made prisoners. Now
the invaders prepared to retreat. By
right of capture the minister was the
property of the three Indians who had
seized and bound him, but one of these
had since been killed. The other two
now took him in charge and fell into

the line of march. Little Eunice was the property of another savage, and no two of the family had for a master the same person. They were all separated. As they left their home they saw that nearly all their neighbors' buildings were in flames and the torch was at once applied to their own house and barn. It was a dreadful experience for all and for none more so than for the seven-year-old Eunice Williams, dragged weeping along by her Indian captor.

As soon as they saw the enemy in retreat the English who had escaped, with such others as had meanwhile come from Hatfield, started in pursuit. A sharp skirmish ensued, in which the assailants lost nine men and were in imminent danger of being all captured. During the fight there was one crisis, when the French commander was so hard pushed that he sent orders to have all the captives tomahawked, but the Indian messenger was fortunately killed before he delivered his orders, and the retreat of the English so soon followed, that the order was not repeated.

Now the three hundred mile march to Canada began in earnest. They crossed the meadow and the river north of the town, and then, at the foot of the mountain, the Indians took away their prisoners' shoes and gave them moccasins to enable them to travel more swiftly.

They made little progress that day, and night overtook them in Greenfield meadows, where they dug away the snow and made some rude wigwams of brush and cut spruce branches for beds. To prevent escapes, Mr. Williams and the other men prisoners were bound, and this continued the practice every night of the journey. During the evening some of the Indians got drunk on the liquors they had brought away from Deerfield and in their orgies they attacked Mr. Williams' negro man and killed him.

Early the next day, when the march was resumed, they found that Green river, near their camping place, barred their way with open water. The stream was swift and the water above knee deep,

but the order was given to wade it. Mrs.
Williams, who was weak from a recent
sickness, stumbled in the midst of the
stream and was plunged entirely under
water. After that, the shock and the
chill made it impossible for her to keep
up with the march, and her Indian captor lifted his hatchet and with one blow
relieved himself of her.

A little later her body was found by
friends who followed that far the line of

the enemy's retreat and they carried
the body back to Deerfield and there
buried it. The stone that marks her

resting-place can be seen to-day in the old burying-ground. If you have patience you can decipher the mossy inscription which reads:

Here lyeth the body of

MRS. EUNICE WILLIAMS,

the vertuous & desirable consort of the Rev'rd. Mr. John Williams, & daughter to ye Rev'rd. Mr. Eleazer & Mrs. Esther Mather of Northampton.

She was born Augt. 2, 1664, and fell by rage of ye barbarous Enemy March 1, 1704.

Prov. 31.28. Her children rise up and call her Blessed.

This incident of Mrs. Williams' death was typical of the prisoners' treatment.

It was the same all through the march —any who became burdensome, sick women, wounded men, or infants in arms, met a quick death and were left to the burial of the sifting winter snows. In the case of the children able to walk some tenderness was shown. The Mohawk who was Eunice's master carried her dryshod across the cold waters of Green river, though when he picked her up she struggled with fear and kicked him fiercely.

Many times afterward when the little girl became too tired to keep up with the rest in the tramp through the drifts, the Indian carried her on his back. She saw other children carried in like manner by their captors, but, it is quite likely, they were moved less by sympathy than by hope of gain. For the children were theirs, and when they reached Canada they could either dispose of them or retain them for their own service.

On the fourth day the army reached the Connecticut river in the vicinity of Brattleboro, and thence northward to White river they traveled on the ice. At the mouth of White river the force was divided and made its way to Canada by several different routes. They had largely to secure their provisions on the march and there were times when they suffered severely from hunger.

Chapter V

Of Eunice Among the Indians in Canada—The
   Jesuits and the Prisoners—Mr. Williams Is
   Allowed to Visit His Daughter—Attempts
   to Redeem Eunice

EUNICE was taken by her captor to his
home at Caughnawaga, the Indian
settlement, nine miles above Montreal.
Her father at length reached the latter
place, and as soon as he learned where
Eunice was held, he begged permission
to see her. This was given reluctantly,
and only at the express command of the
governor, in whom the English found a
considerate foe, if he was not a positive
friend. The dominant influence in control of the child was that of the Indians
and the Jesuit priests by whom this
particular band of Indians had been
converted. No doubt her Indian master
made the white child useful, and it may
be he took a fancy to her that made him
reluctant to part with her for ransom

money.   But there is no question as to
the position of the Jesuits.   They showed
the greatest eagerness for proselyting;
and kidnaping, and threats, and torture
were naught if they could by those
means save souls.   Their power was
always used to retain the children of the
English, to make them forget their earlier impressions and homes, and to adopt
the true religion.

The priests told Mr. Williams that the
Mohawks would as soon part with their
hearts as his child.   The governor had no
power to compel the Indians to surrender
the child, as they were allies rather than
subjects, and the priestly faction was too
powerful for him to directly oppose.

The father's interview with his daughter lasted an hour.   The little girl did
not like her Indian life and cried to be
taken away.   Among other things she
said that the savages did not keep the
Sabbath, and she thought, a few days
before, they "had been mocking the
devil," and these things troubled her
New England conscience greatly.

Her father told her to pray every day and not to forget her catechism or the Scriptures she had learned by heart. In reply the child said that "a tall, lean man in a black gown comes and makes me say some prayers in Latin, but," she added, " I don't understand one word of them; I hope it won't do me any harm."

The interview came to an end and the minister went sadly back to Montreal. The governor made every effort to secure the child's release, but without success. He understood he had the promise of her at one time if he would procure an Indian girl in her stead, and he sent a long distance up the river for one. But when he offered her she was refused. He agreed to pay them a large sum of money, but they said, " No." Finally his lady went over and begged the little girl from the tribe, but all in vain. She staid on, she was dressed as an Indian, she lived as one, and at length she had well-nigh forgotten how to speak English. Three years passed and it was reported that she herself was unwilling to leave the life she had adopted.

Mr. Williams and the others of his family had all been redeemed by the end of 1706. Their period of captivity had not been all hardship. The French, in general, showed them only kindness. Real pity seemed to be felt for the prisoners, and some declared openly that they decried the official methods of conquest. They said that to send the Indians, with their barbaric notions of warfare, against the English was no better than massacre.

With the official class the captives did not fare so well. They found most of them given to intrigue and double dealing. As for the Indians, they were crafty and uncertain, and the priests were apt to be so zealous for the religion of Rome, and so bent on making all the world accept their faith, whether it would or not, that the springs of sympathy were dried up within them. Yet, if the methods of the latter were sometimes unfeeling and cruel, those of the captives in dealing with the priests were not above reproach. Mr. Williams himself was very bumptious on the subject of religion, and was often needlessly irritating in his talk with the Jesuits. He told them openly that they were humbugs and their religion a lie, and that his own New England doctrine was the only true stripe. Nothing would persuade him to enter one of their churches—he would as soon go into a workshop of Satan's. So each party saw things their own way, and each, in the view of the other, was going in obstinacy and blindness straight down the road that led to Sheol.

Mr. Williams, in the final pages of his book, bespeaks the prayers of all New England for the ten-year-old daughter he left behind in Canada. No doubt this request met with wide response. In his own prayers she was remembered as long as he lived, and he never ceased to petition, not only for her release, but for the soul jeopardized by the influence of the priests. It is known also that she was constantly prayed for by her brother, Rev. Stephen Williams of Longmeadow, who was concerned both for her " Spirit-

ual and Eternal Good," and that " God would touch her heart and incline her to turn to her friends."

A few days after Mr. Williams reached Boston from Quebec, he was visited by

a delegation from Deerfield, and in be-
half of the town was entreated to return
to his former parish.   After due deliber-
ation the call was accepted.   A new
house was built for him and in a short
time he married again and the troubled
days of capture and captivity seemed
largely to be laid away in the silence of
the past, out of sight and out of mind.
But he did not forget the daughter in
Canada.

On one occasion, the report was
brought to Deerfield that Eunice Will-
iam's Indian master had promised to
bring her home within two months, but
the two months went by and the captive did not return.

Several years passed and in 1711 an
Indian squaw came timidly into the
heart of Boston and sought the old
Province House. She wished to see the
governor, and she asked of him her children, captured recently and now held in
Boston. The governor thinks and then he
speaks.   He says he will exchange the
children of the woman for Eunice Will-

iams, now held captive by the praying
Mohawks of Caughnawaga.

Forth went the squaw and for many
long summer days she pushed on
through the wilderness toward Montreal. But when she reached her journey's end there was the same old mystery of delay and objection. At last the
offer was made by the French of four
other English prisoners to be given instead of Eunice, and the offer was accepted and the Boston pappooses went
to the mother, and the minister's daughter was still among the Indians.

In 1713, John Schuyler made the journey to Canada in the interest of the
prisoners held there and he took pains
to see Eunice at Caughnawaga with the
hope to bring her away with him. But
he found that she had not only accepted
the faith of the Jesuits and been re-
baptised Margaret, but that she was now
married to a young Indian. She, with
her husband, was brought in to see
Schuyler at the house of one of the
priests. He reports her to have been

looking " very poor in body and bashful in the face."

He desired her to sit down, which she did. First he spoke to her in English, but she did not respond. He thought she could not understand and then employed his Indian "Languister"

to convey what he would say to her. Nevertheless, she would speak not one word. Finally Schuyler asked the priest to talk with her, and beg of her, if she would not return home to stay, at least to go to see her father and afterward return to Canada. But she continued silent until the very last, when, in

response to a final appeal, she said in a
low voice, " Zaghte oghte," which in
English means, " It may not be." Those
words were the only ones she would
vouchsafe in all the two hours Schuyler
spent with her. Schuyler was much
moved, now compassionate, now indig-
nant, and he said to her as he left, " Had
I made such proposals and prayings to
the worst of Indians, I do not doubt but
I would have had a reasonable answer
and consent to what I said."

At this Eunice's husband touched
Schuyler on the arm and said in broken
English, " She no go. Her father
marry twice times. He no have marry,
she go."

Schuyler said no more. He caught
Eunice's limp, unresisting hand within
his two strong brown ones and held it a
moment, then turned on his heel and
hurried away.

Chapter VI

Of the Return of Peace—The Troubles of the
Commission to Secure the Release of the
Captives Held in Canada — Eunice Refuses
to Return—Visits of Eunice and her Descendants to Their Old Home

THE same year Schuyler made his
Canadian journey peace was established between France and England, and
in the autumn orders were received in
America for the release of captives. A
commission was at once appointed by
Governor Dudley of Massachusetts to
go to Canada to hunt up and bring home
the New England people held there.
This commission left Northampton for
Albany on the 9th of November, and
one of the party was Pastor Williams of
Deerfield.

The horseback journey to Albany occupied four days. Here winter came,
with uncertain weeks of cold and thaws
which kept them from proceeding north-

ward till late in December. Then they went on by way of Saratoga and Crown Point, sometimes on snow-shoes, sometimes in canoes. Thus they reached Chambly, whence they proceeded to Quebec in sleighs.

Governor De Vaudrueil gave them his word of honor that all prisoners should have full liberty to return, and told his visitors to go freely among them and send for them to come to their lodgings. The commission were much pleased with their reception, but soon after we find them complaining to the governor that the priests are exerting themselves to prevent the prisoners going. His Excellency replied that he could "as easily alter the course of the waters as prevent the priests' endeavors."

Mr. Williams was no less ardent than the priests, and it was presently forbidden that he should have any religious talk with the captives. He was accused of being abroad after eight o'clock in the evening to discourse on religion with some of the English, and he was told that if he repeated the offense he would be confined a prisoner in his lodgings. The priests affirmed that he undid in a moment all they had done in seven years to establish their religion.

Early in this Canadian trip Mr. Williams had an interview with his daughter, but she would not leave the Indians; and though he pleaded with them, and with the priests and authorities, sometimes so much moved that the tears streamed down his face, they simply said that the girl could go or stay as she chose, and she chose to stay.

After nine months' absence the commission returned, their efforts largely baffled, and with but twenty-six prisoners. No further attempt was made officially for the redemption of Eunice Williams, but in 1740 another interview was had with her, which led to her thrice revisiting the place of her nativity. She came with her husband and others of the tribe, all in Indian costume, and so entirely had she lost her English that it was only by means

of an interpreter that it was possible to
carry on the simplest conversation
with her. It is said, too, that civilized
life was so repugnant to her that she
refused to sleep in her relatives' houses.
The legend is that while visiting her
brother, the minister of Longmeadow,
she persisted in staying with the Indians who pitched their camp in the
woods east of the parsonage. She
was kindly received by her friends,
but all inducements held out to get
her to stay in her old home were una-
vailing. The General Court offered
a grant of land on condition that she
and her husband and children would
remain in New England. She refused
on the ground that it would endanger
her soul.

The die was cast, she had adopted
the life and religion of the North, and
thus she lived a true savage all her
ninety years. If there was an undue
force used earlier, later it was the ties
of family and habit that bound her. It
is understood that her husband adopted

his wife's name and became a Williams, and that their Indian descendants are still a part of the tribe, members in good and regular standing in spite of the fact that they keep the Puritan name.

A company of these Williams Indians visited Deerfield as recently as 1837. There were several families, amounting in all to twenty-three persons. The eldest, a woman of eighty years, affirmed that Eunice was her grandmother. During their stay of a little more than a week they encamped on the village outskirts, and employed their spare time in making baskets. They visited the graves of their ancestors, Rev. John Williams and wife, and attended service on Sunday in an orderly and reverent manner. They refused to receive company on the Sabbath, and at all times and in all respects seemed disposed to conduct themselves decently and inoffensively. Their encampment was frequented by great numbers of persons, almost denying them time to eat their meals, but affording them a ready sale for their baskets.

The descendants of Eunice Williams are Indians still, and still have their home on the banks of the St. Lawrence, and they continue to make the baskets and other simple Indian wares of commerce. It is a strange story, and, as I have said before, the mystery still remains as to whether their white ancestress was a savage from choice or lived her long life in repression and unhappiness.

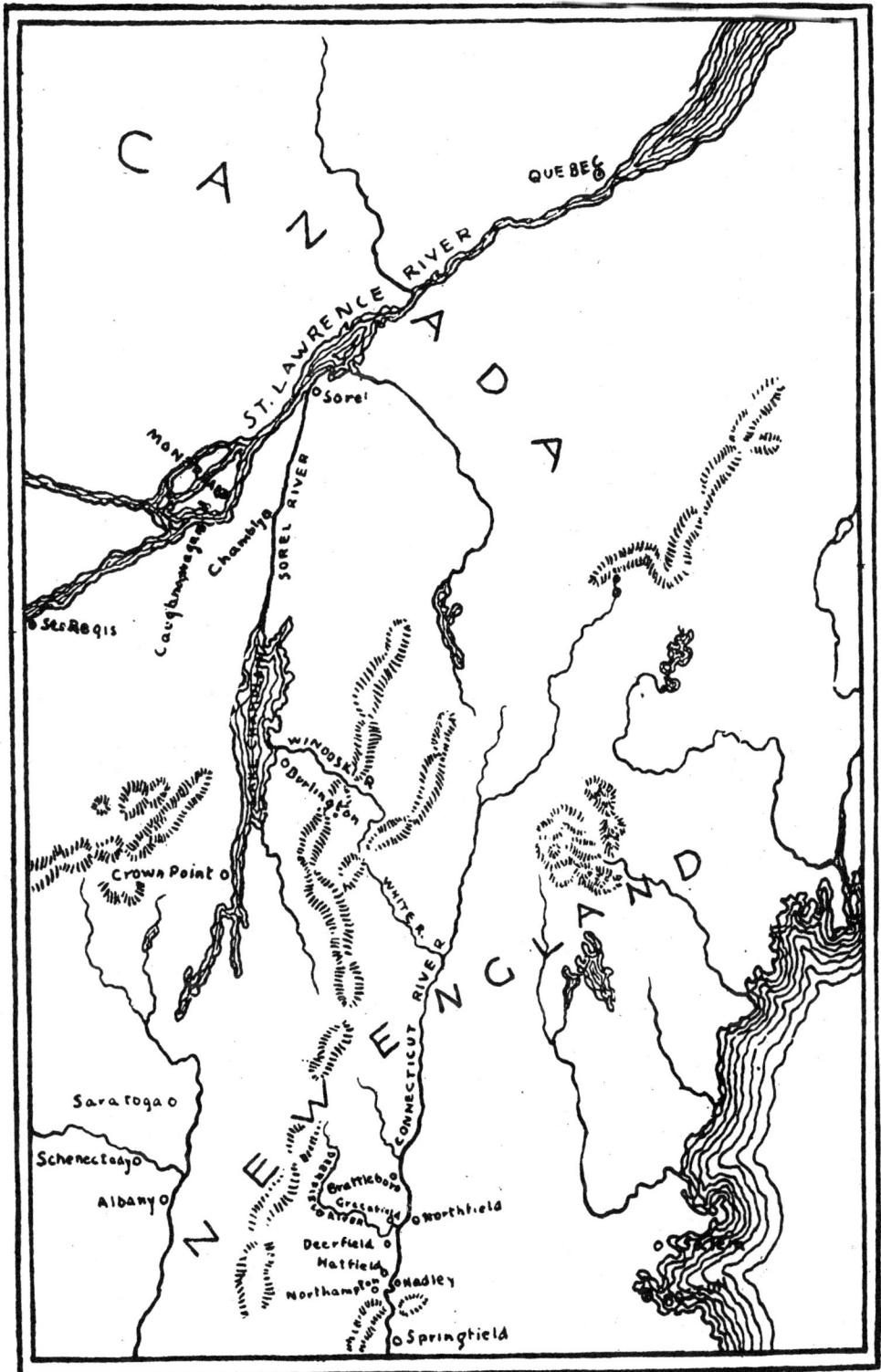

COLOPHON

Clifton Johnson's, *AN UNREDEEMED CAPTIVE*, was printed in the workshop of Glen Adams in Fairfield, Washington. Fairfield is located on State Highway 27 which runs between Opportunity and Tekoa, Washington, and is one township removed from the Idaho border. Additional typesetting for this edition was done by Teresa Ruggles. Photography/film stripping was done by Dustin Newlun who also burned the printing plates. Printing was done by Trevor Del Medico using a Heidelberg press, model KORS. Folding was done by Garry Adams using a 26x40 Baum Dial-O-Matic, three stage folding machine. Adhesive binding was also done by Garry Adams using a Mark II Sulby adhesive binding machine. This is the 702nd title to come from Ye Galleon Press. This was a fun project with no special difficulties.